Editor
Gisela Lee, M.A.

Managing Editor
Karen Goldfluss, M.S. Ed.

Editor-in-Chief
Sharon Coan, M.S. Ed.

Illustrator
Sue Fullam

Cover Artist
Barb Lorseyedi

Art Coordinator
Kevin Barnes

Art Director
CJae Froshay

Imaging
Temo Parra
Rosa C. See

Product Manager
Phil Garcia

Publisher
Mary D. Smith, M.S. Ed.

Practice Makes Perfect

Word Problems

GRADE 6

Author

Robert W. Smith

Teacher Created Resources, Inc.
6421 Industry Way
Westminster, CA 92683
www.teachercreated.com

ISBN: 978-0-7439-3731-3

©2003 Teacher Created Resources, Inc.
Reprinted, 2013
Made in U.S.A.

Table of Contents

Introduction 3

Practice 1: Simple Problems with Whole Numbers 4

Practice 2: Using Code Words/Mixed Operations 5

Practice 3: Using Code Words/Mixed Operations 6

Practice 4: Fractions/Mixed Operations 7

Practice 5: Fractions/Mixed Operations 8

Practice 6: Mixed Numbers/Addition and Subtraction 9

Practice 7: Mixed Numbers/Multiplication and Division 10

Practice 8: Mixed Numbers/Mixed Operations 11

Practice 9: Money 12

Practice 10: Decimals/Addition and Subtraction 13

Practice 11: Decimals/Multiplication and Division 14

Practice 12: Percentages 15

Practice 13: Discounts and Sales Tax 16

Practice 14: Decimals/Mixed Operations 17

Practice 15: Rate Problems 18

Practice 16: Time and Distance 19

Practice 17: Signed Numbers 20

Practice 18: Signed Numbers 21

Practice 19: Single Bar and Double Bar Graphs 22

Practice 20: Single Bar and Double Bar Graphs 23

Practice 21: Single Line and Double Line Graphs 24

Practice 22: Tables, Plots, and Pictographs 25

Practice 23: Problems Involving Distorted or Misleading Data 26

Practice 24: Geometry: Perimeter and Area 27

Practice 25: Geometry: Area 28

Practice 26: Geometry: Circumference 29

Practice 27: Geometry: Area of Circles 30

Practice 28: Geometry: Volume 31

Practice 29: Coordinate Pairs 32

Practice 30: Probability 34

Practice 31: Problems with Equations 35

Practice 32: Ratios 36

Practice 33: Ratios and Proportions 37

Practice 34: Averages 38

Practice 35: Modes and Medians 39

Test Practice 1 40

Test Practice 2 41

Test Practice 3 42

Test Practice 4 43

Test Practice 5 44

Test Practice 6 45

Answer Sheet 46

Answer Key 47

Introduction

The old adage "practice makes perfect" can really hold true for your child and his or her education. The more practice and exposure your child has with concepts being taught in school, the more success he or she is likely to find. For many parents, knowing how to help their children can be frustrating because the resources may not be readily available. As a parent it is also difficult to know where to focus your efforts so that the extra practice your child receives at home supports what he or she is learning in school.

This book has been designed to help parents and teachers reinforce basic skills with their children. *Practice Makes Perfect* reviews basic math skills for children in grade 6. The math focus is word problems. While it would be impossible to include in this book all concepts taught in grade 6, the following basic objectives are reinforced through practice exercises. These objectives support math standards established on district, state, or national levels. (Refer to the Table of Contents for the specific objectives of each practice page.)

- percentages
- adding and subtracting 2-digit numbers
- adding and subtracting 3-digit numbers
- adding and subtracting 4-digit numbers
- adding and subtracting 5- and 6-digit numbers
- multiplying numbers

- tables, graphs, and charts
- choosing operations
- working with money and time
- working with fractions
- basic geometery

There are 35 practice pages organized sequentially so children can build their knowledge from more basic skills to higher-level math skills. To correct the practice pages in this book, use the answer key provided on pages 47 and 48. Six practice tests follow the practice pages. These provide children with multiple-choice test items to help prepare them for standardized tests administered in schools. As a child completes a problem, he or she fills in the correct letter among the answer choices. An optional "bubble-in" answer sheet has also been provided on page 46. This answer sheet is similar to those found on standardized tests. As your child completes each test, he or she can fill in the correct bubbles on the answer sheet.

How to Make the Most of This Book

Here are some useful ideas for optimizing the practice pages in this book:

- Set aside a specific place in your home to work on the practice pages. Keep it neat and tidy with materials on hand.

- Set up a certain time of day to work on the practice pages. This will establish consistency. An alternative is to look for times in your day or week that are less hectic and more conducive to practicing skills.

- Keep all practice sessions with your child positive and constructive. If the mood becomes tense or you and your child are frustrated, set the book aside and look for another time to practice with your child.

- Help with instructions if necessary. If your child is having difficulty understanding what to do or how to get started, work the first problem through with him or her.

- Review the work your child has done. This serves as reinforcement and provides further practice.

- Allow your child to use whatever writing instruments he or she prefers. For example, colored pencils can add variety and pleasure to drill work.

- Pay attention to the areas in which your child has the most difficulty. Provide extra guidance and exercises in those areas. Allowing children to use drawings and manipulatives, such as coins, tiles, game markers, or flash cards, can help them grasp difficult concepts more easily.

- Look for ways to make real-life application to the skills being reinforced.

Practice 1

The students at Garfield School are participating in a marble marathon. There are all kinds of contests and games. Help the students keep track of their marbles.

1. George has a bag with 31 marbles at school but he has 9 times as many marbles at home. How many marbles does he have at home? _____

2. Marissa has 49 marbles and her friend, Alice, has 97 marbles. How many marbles do they have altogether? _____

3. Ashley has 327 marbles in her collection. Amber has 139 marbles. How many more marbles does Ashley have? _____

4. Timothy had 111 marbles. He lost 56 marbles. How many marbles does he have left? _____

5. Laura has 47 marbles. The students in Room 15's fifth grade classroom have 28 times as many marbles as Laura. How many marbles do the students in Room 15 have? _____

6. The 30 students in Room 19 pooled all of their marbles in one giant basket. They had 1,110 marbles in the basket. What was the average number of marbles each child contributed? _____

7. A group of 11 boys won a contest with 1,056 marbles as the prize. They split the marbles evenly among themselves. How many marbles did each boy receive? _____

8. Elaine had 129 marbles on Monday. On Friday she had 351 marbles. How many more marbles did she gain during the week? _____

9. Chad had 512 marbles in his collection. He gave 267 marbles to his best friend. How many marbles did Chad have left? _____

10. Joseph owned 79 marbles. He won a marble shooting contest which had a prize of 389 marbles. How many marbles does Joseph have now? _____

11. Mrs. Shaw's 6th grade class won 2,000 marbles as a reward for their reading. They decided to split the marbles evenly among all 28 students. How many marbles did each student receive? _____. How many marbles were left over? _____

12. A barrel of 2,000 marbles had 569 red marbles and 987 blue marbles. The rest of the marbles were yellow. How many yellow marbles were there? _____

Practice 2 ⟳ ⟲ ⟳ ⟲ ⟳ ⟲ ⟳ ⟲ ⟳ ⟲ ⟳ ⟳ ⟲

Directions: Read each problem. Determine the operation needed to solve it and write the solution in the space provided.

1. In his career, Henry Aaron collected 6,856 total stolen bases, Stan Musial collected 6,134 total bases, and Willie Mays had 6,066 total bases. How many bases did they have altogether?

   Operation: _____   **Solution:** _____

2. In his career, Pete Rose had 14,053 at bats. Henry Aaron had 12,364 at bats. How many more at bats did Pete Rose have?

   Operation: _____   **Solution:** _____

3. Henry Aaron hit 755 career home runs. Babe Ruth hit 714 career home runs. Willie Mays hit 660 career home runs. How many home runs did they hit in all?

   Operation: _____   **Solution:** _____

4. Pete Rose collected 4,256 career hits in 24 years as a major league player. About how many hits did he average per year?

   Operation: _____   **Solution:** _____

5. Bank One Ballpark in Arizona can seat 48,500 people for a game. How many tickets could they sell for 81 games?

   Operation: _____   **Solution:** _____

6. Nolan Ryan had 5,714 lifetime strikeouts against the batters he faced. Steve Carlton had 4,136 lifetime strikeouts. How many more strikeouts did Nolan Ryan have?

   Operation: _____   **Solution:** _____

7. Dodger Stadium in Los Angeles will seat 56,000 fans. How many groups of 20 fans could they fit into Dodger Stadium?

   Operation: _____   **Solution:** _____

8. Babe Ruth had 2,062 career walks. Mickey Mantle collected 1,733 walks. How many fewer walks did Mantle have?

   Operation: _____   **Solution:** _____

9. Ty Cobb had 4,189 hits in a 24 year career. Approximately what was his average number of hits per year?

   Operation: _____   **Solution:** _____

10. The St. Louis Cardinals have won 9 World Series in the 15 World Series they have played. What is their winning percentage?

    Operation: _____   **Solution:** _____

Practice 3 ⋄ ⊚ ⋄ ⊚ ⋄ ⊚ ⋄ ⊚ ⋄ ⊚ ⋄ ⊚ ⋄ ⊚

Directions: Read each problem. Determine the operation needed to solve it and write the solution in the space provided.

1. Dodger Stadium will hold 56,000 fans. Staples Center seats 18,964 Lakers' fans. How many more people can attend a Dodger game?

   Operation: _____ **Solution:** _____

2. The Alamodome in San Antonio has a normal capacity of 20,557 seats for Spurs' fans, but it can seat 35,000 for special events. How many more people can it seat for special events?

   Operation: _____ **Solution:** _____

3. Lambeau Field in Green Bay, Wisconsin seats 60,890 Packers' fans. The Georgia Dome in Atlanta seats 71,228 Falcons' fans. How many fans can be seated altogether in the two parks?

   Operation: _____ **Solution:** _____

4. The Arrowhead Pond in Anaheim will accommodate 17,174 Mighty Ducks' fans. Staples Center will hold 18,118 L. A. Kings' fans. How many can be held altogether in the two arenas?

   Operation: _____ **Solution:** _____

5. The United Center in Chicago will hold 21,500 Bulls' fans. How many 25-seat ticket packages could be sold for one game?

   Operation: _____ **Solution:** _____

6. Comerica Park in Detroit will hold 40,000 Tigers' fans. If tickets to one game were sold in 20-seat packages, how many of these packages could be sold?

   Operation: _____ **Solution:** _____

7. Fenway Park in Boston will hold 33,871 Red Sox fans. Veterans Stadium in Philadelphia will hold 62,409 Phillies' fans. How many more fans can attend a game in Philadelphia?

   Operation: _____ **Solution:** _____

8. The Rams can fit 66,000 fans in their St. Louis Stadium. If all tickets were sold in packages of 8, how many ticket packages could be sold for one game?

   Operation: _____ **Solution:** _____

9. The Miami Dolphins can fit 75,192 fans in their stadium. How many total fans could attend all 8 regular season games?

   Operation: _____ **Solution:** _____

10. Edison Field in Anaheim will hold 45,050 fans. How many tickets could they sell for their 81 regular season games?

    Operation: _____ **Solution:** _____

  #3731 *Practice Makes Perfect: Word Problems*

Practice 4 ⌀ ⌀ ⌀ ⌀ ⌀ ⌀ ⌀ ⌀ ⌀ ⌀ ⌀ ⌀ ⌀ ⌀

Candy Is Dandy is a special candy store with trays of Lick 'em Lollipops, Nutty Buddies, Chocolate P and P's, Jelly Smellies, Luscious Licorice, Geodesic Gumballs, Chocolate-Covered Peanuts, and Slurpy Suckers. Use your knowledge of fractions to help Candy Is Dandy serve its customers.

1. Your mother bought $\frac{1}{3}$ of a pound of Jelly Smellies and $\frac{1}{4}$ of a pound of Geodesic Gumballs. How many pounds of candy did she buy? _____

2. The school principal bought $\frac{3}{4}$ of a pound of Nutty Buddies and the second grade teacher bought $\frac{2}{3}$ of a pound of Nutty Buddies. How many pounds of Nutty Buddies did they buy in all? _____

3. Your best friend bought $\frac{7}{8}$ of a pound of Slurpy Suckers. The school quarterback bought $\frac{3}{4}$ of a pound of Slurpy Suckers. How much more did your friend buy?

   _____

4. The soccer coach bought $\frac{11}{12}$ of a pound of Chocolate-Covered Peanuts. The basketball coach bought $\frac{5}{6}$ of a pound of the same candy. How much more did the soccer coach buy?

   _____

5. Candy is Dandy is selling Chocolate P and P's in baggies which hold $\frac{1}{3}$ of a pound. Robert bought 15 bags of P and P's. How many pounds of candy did he buy?

   _____

6. Chris bought $\frac{3}{4}$ of a foot of Luscious Licorice. James only bought $\frac{1}{3}$ as much licorice as Chris. How much licorice did James buy? _____

7. Christine bought $\frac{9}{10}$ of a pound of P and P's and $\frac{4}{5}$ of a pound of Chocolate-Covered Peanuts. How much candy did she buy altogether? _____

8. Sarah bought $\frac{1}{8}$ of a foot of Luscious Licorice and Angela bought $\frac{7}{12}$ of a foot of licorice. How much less did Sarah buy? _____

9. Anthony bought $\frac{3}{4}$ of a pound of P and P's which he split evenly into cups holding $\frac{1}{8}$ of a pound. How many cups did he have? _____

10. Michael bought $\frac{1}{2}$ pound of Nutty Buddies, $\frac{4}{5}$ of a pound of Geodesic Gumballs, and $\frac{1}{3}$ of a pound of Slurpy Suckers. How many pounds of candy did he buy altogether?

    _____

Practice 5   ꩜ ꩜ ꩜ ꩜ ꩜ ꩜ ꩜ ꩜ ꩜ ꩜ ꩜ ꩜ ꩜ ꩜

A sixth grade science teacher uses many materials which need to be carefully measured and combined. Help compute these fractional measurements for sixth grade science.

1. The teacher needs to distribute $\frac{1}{2}$ ounce of vinegar to each of 30 students. How much vinegar will the teacher need? _____

2. In a class of 33 students, every student will need $\frac{3}{4}$ of an ounce of plain rubbing alcohol. How much alcohol will the teacher need for the entire class? _____

3. Each student will need $\frac{1}{8}$ of an ounce of pepper and $\frac{2}{5}$ of an ounce of salt for a science activity. What is the total weight given to each student? _____

4. The teacher needs to distribute $\frac{1}{2}$ ounce of iron filings to each student from a $12\frac{1}{2}$ ounce jar. How many students can receive iron filings from one jar? _____

5. The teacher has $11\frac{2}{3}$ minutes left in his classroom period. Each student needs $\frac{5}{6}$ of a minute to make a brief presentation. How many students can present in the allotted time?

   _____

6. Each student received $\frac{2}{3}$ of an ounce of flour and $\frac{3}{4}$ of an ounce of baking soda. How much more baking soda did each student receive? _____

7. Each student received $\frac{9}{10}$ of an ounce of glue and $\frac{4}{5}$ of an ounce of water. How much fluid did each individual student receive? _____

8. In one class $\frac{4}{5}$ of an ounce of water was distributed to each of 34 students. How much water was used for the entire class? _____

9. Each student in a class of 25 was given $\frac{3}{8}$ of an ounce of lemon juice to use for invisible writing. How much lemon juice did the teacher distribute? _____

10. Each magnet distributed to a class of 28 students weighed $\frac{5}{16}$ of a pound. How much did all 28 magnets weigh? _____

11. Each student received $\frac{3}{4}$ of an ounce of water, $\frac{2}{3}$ of an ounce of glue, and $\frac{1}{12}$ of an ounce of food coloring. What was the total fluid amount given to each student? _____

12. The teacher divided $24\frac{1}{2}$ ounces of liquid bluing in cups holding $\frac{7}{8}$ ounces. How many cups did the teacher need? _____

Practice 6

Directions: Use your knowledge of mixed numbers to solve these word problems.

1. A house mouse is $7\frac{3}{4}$ inches long. A common rat is $18\frac{1}{8}$ inches long. How much longer is the rat? _____

2. A male long-tailed weasel is $21\frac{3}{4}$ inches long. A female is 11 inches long. What is their combined length? _____

3. A raccoon is $37\frac{3}{8}$ inches long. A porcupine is $36\frac{1}{2}$ inches long. How much shorter is the porcupine? _____

4. A coyote has a body length of $36\frac{1}{8}$ inches and a tail which is $15\frac{1}{2}$ inches long. What is the total length from the tip of the nose to the tip of the tail? _____

5. A New England cottontail rabbit weighs $47\frac{1}{2}$ ounces. A mountain cottontail weighs $36\frac{3}{8}$ ounces. How much do they weigh altogether? _____

6. A male arctic fox weighs $8\frac{3}{4}$ lbs. A female arctic fox weighs $5\frac{1}{2}$ lbs. What is the difference in their weights? _____

7. A female gray fox weighs $7\frac{1}{4}$ lbs. A male gray fox weighs 13 lbs. How much do they weigh altogether? _____

8. A California gray squirrel has a body length of $11\frac{3}{4}$ inches and a tail which is $12\frac{5}{12}$ inches long. What is the total length of the squirrel from the tip of the nose to the tip of the tail?

   _____

9. A male red squirrel weighs $8\frac{7}{8}$ ounces. The female weighs $5\frac{1}{4}$ ounces. How much do they weigh altogether? _____

10. The total length of the black-tailed jack rabbit is $24\frac{3}{4}$ inches. The tail is $4\frac{3}{8}$ inches long. How long is the rest of the body? _____

Practice 7 ⟩ ☙ ⟩ ☙ ⟩ ☙ ⟩ ☙ ⟩ ☙ ⟩ ☙ ⟩ ⟩ ☙

Directions: Use your knowledge of mixed numbers to solve these word problems.

1. Joseph has a footprint which is $9\frac{1}{2}$ inches long from the tip of the shoe to the end of the heel. How many inches long would 8 of his footprints equal? _____

2. Alyssa has a shoeprint which is $5\frac{4}{5}$ inches long. What would be the length of 9 of her shoeprints? _____

3. Laura left a 65-inch line of shoeprints made heel to toe. Her shoe makes a print which is $6\frac{1}{2}$ inches long. How many prints were in the line? _____

4. Robert left a 58-inch line of shoeprints made heel to toe. His shoe makes a print which is $7\frac{1}{4}$ inches long. How many prints were in the line? _____

5. Jorge has a shoeprint which is $8\frac{1}{3}$ inches long. What is the total length of a line of 18 of Jorge's shoeprints? _____

6. Tony leaves a footprint which is $17\frac{3}{4}$ inches long. How long is a line of 20 of his footprints? _____

7. Maria has a footprint which is $6\frac{2}{3}$ inches long. How long a line is made by $3\frac{1}{2}$ of her footprints? _____

8. Aaron's shoeprints made a line $45\frac{1}{2}$ inches long. Each print was $6\frac{1}{2}$ inches long. How many prints were in the line? _____

9. Alex left a line of 22 shoeprints. Each print was $20\frac{1}{2}$ inches long. How long was the line? _____

10. Elaine had a shoeprint of $4\frac{7}{8}$ inches. She left a 39 inch long line of shoeprints. How many shoeprints were in the line? _____

Practice 8

The sixth grade students at Garfield School participated in a roller derby contest. Each car in the contest rolled down a ramp onto the floor until it stopped. Help the contestants compute the distances their cars traveled.

1. Roland's roller derby car traveled $4\frac{1}{2}$ feet past the bottom of the ramp. Eleanor's car traveled $6\frac{3}{4}$ feet past the ramp. How much farther did Eleanor's car travel? _____

2. Josh raced two cars. His first one traveled $5\frac{1}{2}$ feet past the ramp. His second car traveled $4\frac{1}{3}$ feet past the ramp. How far did they travel in all? _____

3. Jolene's three-wheeler traveled $8\frac{1}{2}$ feet down the ramp and $9\frac{1}{4}$ feet past the ramp. What was the total distance it traveled? _____

4. Maggie's roller derby truck model traveled $2\frac{1}{2}$ feet past the ramp. Victor's car traveled $1\frac{1}{4}$ times as far past the ramp. How far did Victor's car travel? _____

5. Larry's model went $9\frac{1}{3}$ foot past the ramp. Aaron's model went only $\frac{1}{4}$ as far past the ramp. How far did Aaron's model travel? _____

6. Kevin's bottle car was $\frac{5}{6}$ of a foot long. It traveled $5\frac{1}{3}$ feet. How many times would the length of his car divide into the distance he traveled? _____

7. Donavan's boxcar racer was $\frac{5}{8}$ of a foot long. The racer traveled $7\frac{1}{2}$ feet past the ramp. How many boxcar lengths could divide into the distance it traveled past the ramp?

   _____

8. Irene's three-wheeled racer traveled $9\frac{1}{8}$ feet. Her four-wheeler traveled only $\frac{2}{3}$ as far. How many feet did her four-wheeler travel? _____

9. Veronica's miniature racer traveled $3\frac{7}{16}$ feet from the bottom of the ramp. Her full-sized car traveled $1\frac{3}{5}$ times as far from bottom of ramp. How far did the full-sized car travel?

   _____

10. Jorge's first car went $4\frac{1}{2}$ feet. His second traveled $3\frac{1}{3}$ feet. His third entry traveled $6\frac{3}{4}$ feet. How far did they travel altogether? _____

Practice 9

Directions: Forty-one Flavors is a very popular new ice-cream parlor. Here is their menu. Help them compute their sales.

Single Scoop	$1.29	Regular Sundae	$2.79
Double Scoop	$1.69	Large Sundae	$3.29
Triple Scoop	$1.99	Super Sundae	$3.95
Quadruple Scoop	$2.25	Cola Float	$2.90

Remember: All answers involving money must have a dollar sign and a decimal point.

1. Your best friend bought a regular sundae and a quadruple scoop. How much money did he spend? ________________
2. You bought a double scoop and your coach bought a quadruple scoop. How much more did the coach spend? ________________
3. Your teacher bought 32 triple scoops for her fellow teachers. How much money did she spend? ________________
4. The soccer coach bought 11 super sundaes for the team. How much money did it cost the coach? ________________
5. A group of 9 teenagers had a bill for $49.59 at Forty-one Flavors. They decided to split the cost evenly. How much did it cost each person? ________________
6. A team of 12 basketball players had a bill of $60.48 at Forty-one Flavors. They decided to split the cost evenly. How much did each player spend? ________________
7. Your mother bought 13 quadruple scoops for a birthday party. How much was her bill? ________________
8. How much less does it cost to buy a single scoop than a quadruple scoop? ________________
9. What is the total cost of a single scoop, a triple scoop, a super sundae, and a cola float? ________________
10. How much would it cost to buy one of everything on the menu? ________________
11. What is the total cost of 3 quadruple scoops and 4 cola floats? ________________
12. What is the total cost of 5 single scoops, 3 double scoops, and 2 regular sundaes? ________________

Practice 10

Directions: Use your decimal skills to answer these questions.

1. A big-bend gecko is 16.8 centimeters long. A yellow-headed gecko is 8.9 centimeters long. How much longer is the big-bend gecko? _____

2. A gray-banded kingsnake is 120.7 centimeters long. A common kingsnake is 208.3 centimeters long. How much longer is the common kingsnake? _____

3. A green water snake is 187.75 centimeters long. A plain-bellied water snake is 157.5 centimeters long. How much shorter is the plain-bellied water snake? _____

4. A tiger rattlesnake is 91.39 centimeters long. A Mojave rattlesnake is 129.5 centimeters long. What is their combined length? _____

5. One Western rattlesnake is 162.6 centimeters long. Another of the same species is 41.66 centimeters long. What is their combined length? _____

6. One brown water snake is 175.3 centimeters long, another is 71.23 centimeters long, and a third is 101.333 centimeters long. What is the total length of the three snakes? _____

7. An Eastern hognose snake is 114.49 centimeters long. A western hognose snake is 89.5 centimeters long. What is the difference in length? _____

8. A many-lined skunk is 19.399 centimeters long. A prairie skunk is 20.6 centimeters long. What is the difference in length? _____

9. A racerunner is 26.7 centimeters long. A New Mexican whiptail is 30.199 centimeters long. What is their combined length? _____

10. One Western fence lizard is 15.222 centimeters long. Another is 23.444 centimeters long. A third is 20.997 centimeters long. What is their total length? _____

11. A chuckwalla is 41.889 centimeters long. A short-horned lizard is 14.9 centimeters. How much longer is the chuckwalla? _____

12. A common iguana is 200 centimeters long. A Texas-horned lizard is 18.09 centimeters long. How much longer is the iguana? _____

Practice 11 ꙮ ꙮ ꙮ ꙮ ꙮ ꙮ ꙮ ꙮ ꙮ ꙮ ꙮ ꙮ ꙮ ꙮ

Sweet Buggy Bites is a company that creates unusual kinds of candy. They make chocolate-covered ants, grasshopper kisses, sweet 'n sour crickets, beetle bites, and other candy-coated bugs. Use your knowledge of multiplication and division with decimals to compute these answers.

Reminders

- Count all of the places to the right of the decimal in the multiplication problems and have the same number of places to the right of the decimal in the answer.

  Example: $3.1 \times 0.4 = 1.24$

- If the divisor has a decimal, move it to the right of the divisor and move the decimal in the dividend the same number of places to the right.

  Example: $.12\overline{)24.36}$ to $12.\overline{)2436.}$
  $= 203$

---

1. A bag of beetle bites weighs 1.47 lbs. There are 7 candies in each bag. How much does each bite weigh? _____

2. A box of chocolate-coated ants weighs 8.35 ounces. How much do 12 boxes weigh?

   _____

3. A bag of sweet 'n sour crickets weighs 9.81 ounces and holds 9 candies. How much does each candy weigh? _____

4. A large box of grasshopper kisses weighs 18.36 ounces. Each candy weighs 1.8 ounces. How many candies are in the box? _____

5. A super-sized bag of beetle bites weighs 2.255 lbs. What is the weight of 20 bags?

   _____

6. A mini-box of chocolate-covered ants weighs 4.025 ounces. Each ant weighs .05 ounces. How many chocolate-covered ants are in each box? _____

7. A large box of sweet 'n sour crickets weighs 13.467 ounces. How much do 72 boxes weigh?

   _____

8. A regular box of grasshopper kisses costs $4.83 for 21 candies. What is the cost for each candy?

   _____

9. A regular box of sweet 'n sour crickets costs $9.50 for 25 candied crickets. What is the cost for each cricket? _____

10. A box of beetle bites weighs 1.095 lbs. How much does a carton of 144 boxes weigh?

    _____

Practice 12 ꩜ ꩜ ꩜ ꩜ ꩜ ꩜ ꩜ ꩜ ꩜ ꩜ ꩜ ꩜ ꩜

Reminders

- Shooting percentages in basketball are calculated by dividing the number of attempted shots into the number of shots made.
- Passing percentages in football are calculated by dividing the number of attempted passes into the number of completed passes.
- Winning percentages are calculated by dividing the total number of games into the number of games won.
- You need to add a decimal point and 2 or 3 zeroes before dividing.

Directions: Calculate the percentages in each problem below. The first one is done for you.

1. Your best basketball player attempted 20 shots and made 15. Calculate his shooting percentage.

$$
\begin{array}{r}
.75 = 75\% \\
20\overline{)15.00} \\
\underline{14.0} \\
1.00 \\
\underline{100}
\end{array}
$$

2. A shooting guard on your school basketball team attempted 25 shots and made 18. What was the player's shooting percentage? _____

3. The local school quarterback attempted 12 passes and completed 9 passes. What was the quarterback's passing percentage? _____

4. The local school's soccer team played 10 games and won 6 games. What was the team's winning percentage? _____

5. The local school's basketball team had a 24-game season and won 18 games. What was the team's winning percentage? _____

6. The local school's football team played 10 games and won 8 games. What was its winning percentage? _____

7. Joe is the quarterback of the intramural team. He attempts 25 passes and completes 16 passes. What is his passing percentage? _____

8. The girls' softball team played 15 games and won 10 games. What is the team's winning percentage? _____

9. The center on your basketball team attempted 40 shots and made 28 shots. What was the center's shooting percentage? _____

10. The school baseball team played 28 games and won 23 games. What was its winning percentage?

_____

Practice 13

Scooters Galore sells scooters, skateboards, mountain bikes, ten-speed bicycles, rolling shoes, and even pogo sticks. If you can stand on it and ride, they have it. Help compute the discounts and sales tax for their customers.

Reminders

- Discounts are subtracted from the cost.
- Sales tax is added to the cost.

1. Roxanne bought a Lazermatic motorized scooter priced at $169.98. She was given a 20% discount. How much money did she save? ________________

2. Annette bought a Slasher scooter priced at $39.95 before a 10% discount. How much money did she save? ________________

3. Frank bought a Bounce High pogo stick for $16.50. The sales tax was 8%. How much did the tax add to the cost of the pogo stick? ________________

4. Irene purchased a trail bike for $118.95. How much did the 8% sales tax add to the cost of the trail bike? ________________

5. Anthony bought a Powerboard skateboard priced at $28. There was a 25% discount on this board. How much money did he save? ________________

6. Thomas bought a pair of Racer roller shoes for $31. How much more did the 8% sales tax cost him? ________________

7. Tony's little brother got a $38 boy's bike at a 40% discount. How much money did he save? ________________

8. Audrey bought a Double-Tough scooter for $50. How much did the 8% sales tax add to the cost? ________________

9. Matthew bought a $60 Slasher scooter and received a 30% discount. How much did he save with the discount? ________________. What was the actual cost of the scooter? ________________

10. Crystal bought some Super Size rolling shoes for $34.95. She received a 15% discount. How much did she save with the discount? ________________. What was the actual cost of the rolling shoes? ________________

Practice 14 ᗯ ᕮ ᗯ ᕮ ᗯ ᕮ ᗯ ᕮ ᗯ ᕮ ᗯ ᕮ ᗯ ᕮ ᗯ

The technicians who test cars keep very careful records of the performance of each car. Use your knowledge of decimal operations to compare the results for each car tested.

1. A station wagon traveled 248.9 miles on a tank of gas. A sedan traveled 218.576 miles on a tank of gas. How far did they travel altogether? _____

2. A hybrid car is powered by a combination of electrical batteries and gasoline. This vehicle traveled 112.34 miles on one gallon of gasoline. How many miles would it travel on 20 gallons of gasoline? _____

3. The stopping distance for the Laser Racer was 45.678 feet. The stopping distance for the Super Sport was 78.1 feet. What is the difference? _____

4. A regular gasoline-powered car traveled exactly 18.2 miles on a gallon of gasoline. The hybrid car went 112.34 miles on a gallon of gas. How much farther did the hybrid car travel on one gallon? _____

5. The New Wave Motor Company has developed an SUV which travels 380.75 miles on 25 gallons of gasoline. How far can it travel on 1 gallon of gasoline? _____

6. A sports car traveled 198.764 miles on one tank of gas. A sedan traveled 243.4 miles on one tank of gas. How much farther did the sedan travel? _____

7. The maximum speed of a battery-powered vehicle was 42.387 miles per hour. The maximum speed of a gasoline-powered roadster was 220.2 miles per hour. How much faster was the roadster? _____

8. A classic car from the 1960s weighed 4,173.96 pounds. A battery-powered experimental vehicle weighed 1,143.003 pounds. How much heavier was the classic car? _____

9. An experimental car traveled 819.45 miles on 9 gallons of gas. How far did it travel on 1 gallon of gas? _____

10. An experimental motorcycle can travel 189.34 miles on a gallon of gas. How far could it travel on a full tank holding 4.65 gallons of gas? _____

Practice 15 ꩜ ꩜ ꩜ ꩜ ꩜ ꩜ ꩜ ꩜ ꩜ ꩜ ꩜ ꩜

Reminders

- To determine the rate of speed, divide the distance traveled by the time it took to travel that distance.
- The formula is: $r = \dfrac{d}{t}$
- The answer is usually expressed in miles per hour (m.p.h.).

Directions: Compute the rate in each of these problems.

1. Your family took a 360-mile automobile trip from Los Angeles to San Francisco in 6 hours. What was your average speed in miles per hour? _____ m.p.h.

2. The Clark family drove 3,000 miles from New York to Los Angeles in 60 hours of driving. What was their average rate? _____ m.p.h.

3. The Brown family traveled 990 miles from Atlanta, Georgia to Houston, Texas in 33 hours. What was their average rate of speed? _____ m.p.h.

4. Mark's mother drove 2,340 miles from Cincinnati, Ohio to Portland, Oregon in 39 hours. What was her average rate of speed? _____ m.p.h.

5. Shannon's father drove 2,750 miles from Seattle, Washington to Philadelphia, Pennsylvania in 55 hours. What was his average speed in miles per hour? _____ m.p.h.

6. Michelle's family drove 2,200 miles from Houston, Texas to Portland, Oregon in 40 hours. What was their average rate of speed? _____ m.p.h.

7. Alyssa's family drove 3,090 miles from San Francisco, California to Boston, Massachusetts in 60 hours. What was their average speed? _____ m.p.h.

8. Frank's dad drove 1,600 miles from Minneapolis, Minnesota to Seattle, Washington in 40 hours. What was his average speed in miles per hour? _____ m.p.h.

9. Stacy's mother drove 1,040 miles from Denver, Colorado to Memphis, Tennessee in 26 hours. What was her average speed? _____ m.p.h.

10. Jake's dad flew a plane 200 miles from Kansas City, Missouri to Omaha, Nebraska in 2.5 hours. What was the plane's average speed? _____ m.p.h.

Practice 16 ᕙ ᕗ ᕙ ᕗ ᕙ ᕗ ᕙ ᕗ ᕙ ᕗ ᕙ ᕗ ᕙ ᕙ ᕗ

The community park is sponsoring a ride-athon. People can bring their bicycles, skateboards, scooters, or skates. Help compute time and distance for the riders.

Reminders

- Time is computed by dividing the distance traveled by the rate of speed. $t = \dfrac{d}{r}$

- Distance is computed by multiplying the rate of speed times the amount of time expended. $d = rt$

---

1. Kyle rode his skateboard 40 minutes at an average speed of 80 feet per minute. What distance did your friend travel? _____ feet

2. Ashley rode her skateboard 3,200 feet at 80 feet per minute. How many minutes did she ride? _____ minutes

3. The school principal rode her bicycle for 50 minutes at an average speed of 200 feet per minute. How many feet did she travel? _____ feet

4. Jeffrey rode his in-line skates for 99 minutes at an average speed of 72 feet per minute. What distance did Jeffrey travel? _____ feet

5. Veronica rode her motorized scooter 31,680 feet at an average speed of 80 feet per minute. How many minutes did she ride her scooter? _____ minutes

6. Gavin rode his scooter 86 feet per minute for 90 minutes. How many feet did he ride? _____ feet

7. Marie rode her mountain bike for 240 minutes at an average speed of 100 feet per minute. How far did she ride? _____ feet

8. Louise rode her scooter 40,240 feet at 80 feet per minute. How many minutes did she ride her scooter? _____ minutes

9. Jonathan skated 32,800 feet at 80 feet per minute. How many minutes did he skate? _____ minutes

10. Kristin rode her bicycle 320 minutes at 95 feet per minute. How many feet did she ride? _____ feet

---

Practice 17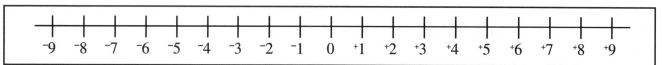

Directions: Compute the positive and negative values indicated in the problems below. Use the number line to help you with the easier amounts. Remember, always start at 0. Go to the right for positive values. Go to the left for negative values.

⁻9	⁻8	⁻7	⁻6	⁻5	⁻4	⁻3	⁻2	⁻1	0	⁺1	⁺2	⁺3	⁺4	⁺5	⁺6	⁺7	⁺8	⁺9

1. You have no money. You owe $4 to your best friend. You earn $5 doing chores. How much money will you have after you pay your friend? _____

2. John has no money and he owes $9 to his brother. He receives $10 for his birthday. How much money does he have after paying back his brother? _____

3. Elizabeth has no money. She owes $7 to Michelle and $4 to Christine. How much money does she owe altogether? _____

4. What is the sum of ⁻9 and ⁺16? _____

5. James has no money and he owes $9 to Ronny and $12 to Melissa. How much money does he owe altogether? _____

6. What is the sum of ⁻10 and ⁺12? _____

7. Irene has $15 but she owes $21 to her friend. How much money will she still owe if she gives the money that she has to her friend? _____

8. What is the sum of ⁻7 and ⁻17? _____

9. George scored 9 points in one game and 8 points in a second game. What was his point total? _____

10. What is the sum of ⁻30 and ⁻42? _____

11. What is the sum of ⁻19 and ⁻13? _____

12. Allison owes $87 to the bank and $139 to the credit card company. How much money does she owe altogether? _____

Practice 18

Directions: Compute the positive and negative values indicated in the problems below.

> ## Reminders
> - A negative times a negative is a positive.
> - A positive times a negative is a negative.
> - A negative divided by a negative is a positive.
> - A positive divided by a negative is a negative.
> - A negative divided by a positive is a negative.

1. Jill owes $4 to Jennifer, $4 to Michelle, and $4 to Eileen. How much does she owe altogether?

   _____

2. Joey owes $5 to 4 different friends. How much money does he owe altogether? _____

3. What is the product of $^-7$ and $^-6$? _____

4. The total bill at a restaurant was $49 to be split evenly among 7 friends. How much money did each friend owe? _____

5. How much is $^-81$ divided by 9? _____

6. How much is $^-100$ divided by $^-10$? _____

7. A group of 18 patrons each owe $15 at a restaurant. What is the total amount owed by all 18 customers? _____

8. What is the product of $^-12$ and $^-13$? _____

9. How much is $^-16$ times 4? _____

10. What is the quotient when $^-45$ is divided by $^-9$? _____

11. A group of 15 teenagers owes $75 at a pizza parlor. If they split the bill evenly, how much will each person owe? _____

12. How much is $^-200$ divided by $^-10$? _____

Practice 19

This single bar graph illustrates the life spans of various animals. Study the graph and use the information to answer the questions below.

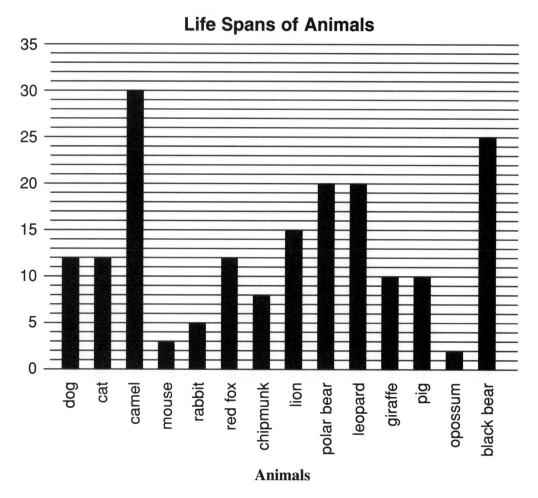

Life Spans of Animals

Animals

1. Which animal on the graph has the longest life span? _____

2. Which three animals live about 12 years? _____

3. How many more years does a black bear live than a polar bear? _____

4. Which animal lives as long as a giraffe? _____

5. How much longer does a leopard live than a mouse? _____

6. How long does a lion live? _____

7. How much longer does a red fox live than a chipmunk? _____

8. How much longer does a cat live than a mouse? _____

9. The average life span of an American is about 75 years. How much longer does a person live than a polar bear? _____

10. How much longer does a person live than a rabbit? _____

Practice 20 ๑ ๑ ๑ ๑ ๑ ๑ ๑ ๑ ๑ ๑ ๑ ๑ ๑

This double bar graph illustrates a survey of the relative popularity of soccer and football as participant sports for boys in the third through the eighth grade.

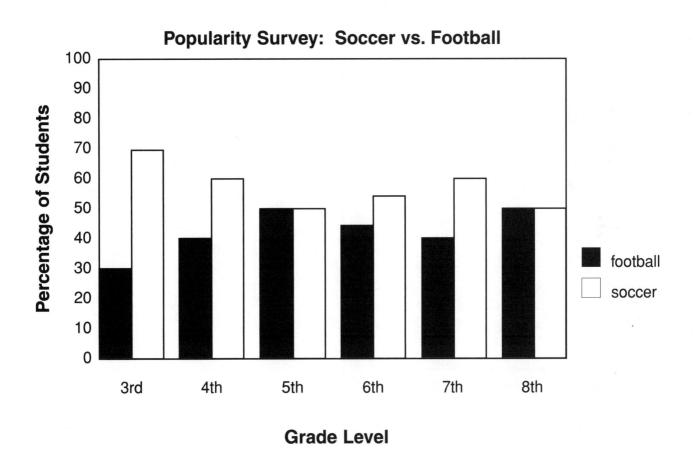

1. What percentage of third grade boys preferred to play football? _____

2. In which two grades do boys like to play soccer and football equally well? _____

3. What percentage of boys in the fourth grade prefer soccer? _____

4. Is there any grade in which more boys prefer football? _____

5. What percentage of boys prefer football in the sixth grade? _____

6. What percentage of boys prefer football in the seventh grade? _____

Practice 21

This single line graph illustrates the percentage of children in the general population from 1950 until 2000. Study the graph and use the information to answer the questions below.

Population of Children in the U.S.

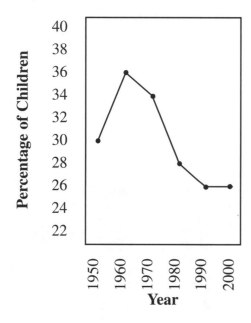

1. In which year did children comprise 36% of the population? _____

2. In which years were only 26% of the population children? _____

3. What year saw the highest percentage of children? _____

4. In which ten-year period did the number of children as a percentage of the population rise? _____

5. In which years are children just about one-fourth of the population? _____

6. In which ten-year period did the greatest drop occur? _____

7. In which ten-year period were children more than one third of the population? _____

8. Does the most recent trend seem to be rising, falling or staying the same? _____

This double line graph shows the average heights of boys and girls by age from 7 through 16. Study the graph and answer the questions below.

Average Heights of Children

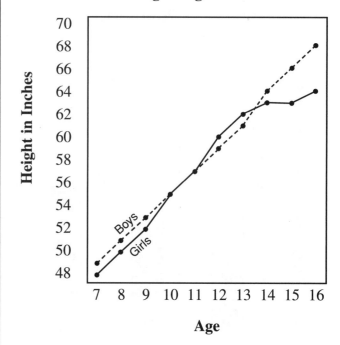

9. At which two ages do boys and girls average the same heights? _____

10. At which two ages are girls on average taller than boys? _____

11. At what age do boys average 4 inches taller than girls? _____

12. At what three ages do boys and girls grow at about the same amount before the girls catch up to boys? _____

13. Are sixth grade girls usually taller or shorter than boys? _____

14. At what age do boys catch up and pass girls? _____

Practice 22 ⟳ ⟳ ⟳ ⟳ ⟳ ⟳ ⟳ ⟳ ⟳ ⟳ ⟳ ⟳ ⟳

This line plot illustrates a survey of hours spent during one week on computer generated games by 29 sixth grade students in one classroom. Study the plot and answer the questions below.

```
Number of Students
X
X                              X
X              X               X
X X            X               X
X X X          X         X   X X   X
X X X X    X X     X     X     X X     X
0          5         10          15
```
Hours Spent Weekly

Note: Each X represents one student.

1. How many students did not spend any time playing computer games? _____

2. How many students spent 3 hours a week playing computer games? _____

3. How many students spent 5 hours a week playing computer games? _____

4. How many students spent 15 hours a week playing computer games? _____

5. How many students spent 10 hours a week playing computer games? _____

6. How many students in the class spent 10 hours or more a week on games? _____

7. How many students in the class spent less than 10 hours a week on games? _____

8. How many students spent 13 hours a week on games? _____

This frequency table illustrates a survey of pets owned by sixth grade students in one classroom. Study the table, complete the frequency totals, and answer the questions below.

Survey of Pets Owned by Sixth Grade Students

Pets	Tally	Frequency
Cat	////////	8
Dog	////////////	
Snake	//	
Bird	///	
Mouse	///	
Hamster	////	
Fish	//////	
Other	///	

9. How many more dogs are owned than cats? _____

10. What is the most frequently owned pet? _____

11. What is the least frequently owned pet? _____

12. How many more cats are owned than mice? _____

13. What is the total number of pets owned by these students? _____

14. How many four-legged animals are owned? _____

Problems Involving Distorted or Misleading Data

Practice 23

This bar graph illustrates the speeds of several animals in miles per hour. Study the graph and answer the questions below.

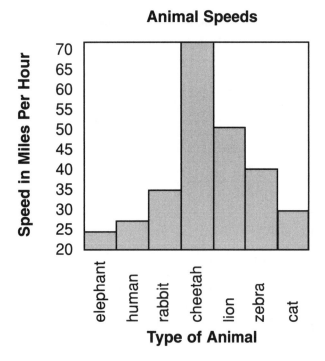

Animal Speeds

1. How much faster is a lion than a cat?
   _____

2. The bar graph makes it look as if the lion is 3 times faster than the cat. Why does it look like that? _____

3. Is a cat 2 times as fast as an elephant?
   _____

4. How much faster is a cat than an elephant?
   _____

5. How much faster than a rabbit is a cheetah?
   _____

6. How does the graph distort the data and make it look as if the cheetah was 2 times as fast as a rabbit? _____

7. How could the scale of the graph be changed to make it less distorted?
   _____

This line graph illustrates average income for a group of people over 7 years. Study the graph. Decide how the graph could be misinterpreted. Answers the questions below.

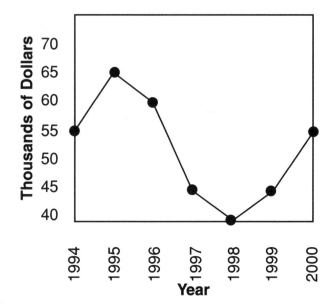

Average Income During a Seven Year Span

8. In which year did the average reach its highest point? _____

9. In which year did the average reach its lowest point? _____

10. How much more did the average person earn in 2000 than in 1999? _____

11. Why does the graph make it appear that income tripled from 1999 to 2000?
    _____

12. What is the difference between the highest yearly income and the lowest yearly income? _____

13. How is the graph distorted or misleading?
    _____

14. How could the distortion be corrected?
    _____

Practice 24 ❧ ❧ ❧ ❧ ❧ ❧ ❧ ❧ ❧ ❧ ❧ ❧ ❧

Many sports require a rectangular field of play which is a specific length and width. Use the information given in the problems below to compute the perimeter and area of each field of play.

> ## Reminder
> - The perimeter of a rectangle is computed by adding the length and width and multiplying by 2.
> - The area of a rectangle is computed by multiplying the length times the width.
>
> Remember: P = (l + w) x 2 and A = l x w

1. An NFL playing field (not counting the end zones) is 300 feet long and 160 feet wide.

   What is the perimeter? _____ What is the area? _____

2. An NBA basketball court is 94 feet long and 50 feet wide.

   What is the perimeter? _____ What is the area? _____

3. A major league baseball diamond is a square 90 feet long on each side.

   What is the perimeter? _____ What is the area? _____

4. An ice hockey rink is 100 feet wide and 200 feet long.

   What is the perimeter? _____ What is the area? _____

5. A field hockey playing area is 100 yards long and 60 yards wide.

   What is the perimeter? _____ What is the area? _____

6. A softball diamond is a square 65 feet long on each side.

   What is the perimeter? _____ What is the area? _____

7. A soccer field is 73 meters wide and 100 meters long.

   What is the perimeter? _____ What is the area? _____

8. The playing area of a Canadian football field (not counting the end zones) is 110 yards long and 65 yards wide.

   What is the perimeter? _____ What is the area? _____

Practice 25

Lawn Magic is a business run by three sixth grade friends who earn money mowing their neighbors' lawns. They charge by the square foot so they need to know the area of each lawn they mow. Help Lawn Magic compute the area in square feet of each lawn described below.

> **Formulas to Remember**
> - Area of a rectangle = base times height (or length times width)
> - Area of a parallelogram = base times height
> - Area of a triangle = base times height divided by 2.

1. Lawn Magic did your neighbor's lawn which is a rectangular shape 12 feet high and 20 feet long at the base. What is the area? _____ square feet

2. Lawn Magic mowed Mr. Crick's parallelogram-shaped lawn which has a height of 15 feet and a base of 30 feet. What is the area? _____ square feet

3. Mr. Ford's lawn is a parallelogram with a height of 23 feet and a base of 45 feet. What is the area Lawn Magic will mow? _____ square feet

4. Mrs. Jopp's lawn is triangular with a height of 12 feet and a base of 40 feet. What is the area that Lawn Magic will mow? _____ square feet

5. Lawn Magic mowed Mr. Lee's front lawn which is a rectangle 43 feet high and 97 feet at the base. What is the area they mowed? _____ square feet

6. Mr. Dapper's back lawn is a triangle with a height of 33 feet and a base of 70 feet. What is the area? _____ square feet

7. Mrs. Smith's side lawn is a parallelogram 22.4 feet high and 30 feet at the base. What is the area Lawn Magic will mow? _____ square feet

8. Lawn Magic mowed Ms. Brown's front lawn, a triangle 12.5 feet high and 14 feet at the base. What is the area they mowed? _____ square feet

9. What is the area of a triangular lawn 16.6 feet high and 12 feet at the base? _____ square feet

10. What is the area of a square lawn 22 feet on each side? _____ square feet

Practice 26 ꩜ ꩜ ꩜ ꩜ ꩜ ꩜ ꩜ ꩜ ꩜ ꩜ ꩜ ꩜ ꩜ ꩜

The circumference of a circle is computed by multiplying the diameter times pi or by doubling the radius and multiplying times pi. ($\pi = 3.14$)

The formulas are: C = πd and C = 2 πr

Directions: Compute the circumference of each circle described below. Use C = πd if the diameter is given. Use C = 2 πr if the radius is given. The first one is done for you.

1. A coaster has a diameter of 9 centimeters. What is the circumference?

   Formula: _____ C = πd _____

   Equation: ___ C = 3.14 x 9 ___

   Answer: ___ C = 28.26 centimeters ___

2. A paper plate has a diameter of 23 centimeters. What is the circumference?

   Formula: _____

   Equation: _____

   Answer: _____

3. A sticker has a radius of 5 centimeters. What is the circumference?

   Formula: _____

   Equation: _____

   Answer: _____

4. A nickel has a diameter of 2 centimeters. What is the circumference?

   Formula: _____

   Equation: _____

   Answer: _____

5. A Susan B. Anthony dollar has a diameter of 2.6 centimeters. What is the circumference?

   Formula: _____

   Equation: _____

   Answer: _____

6. A car wheel has a radius of 12 inches. What is the circumference?

   Formula: _____

   Equation: _____

   Answer: _____

7. A roll of masking tape has a 2-inch radius. What is the circumference?

   Formula: _____

   Equation: _____

   Answer: _____

8. The base of a water bottle has a radius of 3 centimeters. What is the circumference?

   Formula: _____

   Equation: _____

   Answer: _____

Practice 27

To compute the area of a circle, first multiply the radius times itself. Then multiply the product by pi (3.14).

Formula: $A = \pi r^2$

Directions: Compute the area of each of these circles described below. The first one is done for you.

1. A garden planter has a radius of 3 feet. What is the area?

   Formula: $\underline{A = \pi r^2}$

   Equation: $\underline{A = 3 \times 3 \times 3.14}$

   Answer: $\underline{28.26 \text{ cm}^2}$

2. A hubcap has a radius of 8 inches. What is the area of the hubcap?

   Formula: $\underline{A = \pi r^2}$

   Equation: _____

   Answer: _____

3. A CD has a radius of 6 centimeters. What is the area?

   Formula: $\underline{A = \pi r^2}$

   Equation: _____

   Answer: _____

4. A button has a radius of 7 millimeters. What is the area?

   Formula: _____

   Equation: _____

   Answer: _____

5. A penny has a radius of 9 millimeters. What is the area?

   Formula: _____

   Equation: _____

   Answer: _____

6. A plastic wading pool has a radius of 2 feet. What is the area?

   Formula: _____

   Equation: _____

   Answer: _____

7. A circular flower planter has a radius of 4 feet. What is the area?

   Formula: _____

   Equation: _____

   Answer: _____

8. A jar lid has a radius of 4.5 centimeters. What is the area?

   Formula: _____

   Equation: _____

   Answer: _____

9. A clock face has a radius of 3.5 centimeters. What is the area?

   Formula: _____

   Equation: _____

   Answer: _____

10. A quarter has a radius of 1.15 centimeters. What is the area?

    Formula: _____

    Equation: _____

    Answer: _____

Practice 28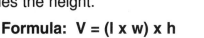

Everything made in The Cubic Factory is in the shape of a cube.

They sell cubic puzzles, cubic games, cubic calendars, and even cubic books. Help the factory package its unusual products.

Reminders

- A cube has the same length, width, and height.
- The volume of a figure is computed by multiplying the length times the width times the height.

Formula: V = (l x w) x h

---

1. The cubic factory sells a giant cubic puzzle which is 6 inches long, 6 inches wide, and 6 inches high. What is the volume of the puzzle in cubic inches? _____

2. The factory sells cubic puzzles which are 3 centimeters long, 3 centimeters wide, and 3 centimeters high. What is the volume of the puzzle in cubic centimeters? _____

3. One cubic board game is 9 inches high, 9 inches wide, and 9 inches long. What is the volume in cubic inches? _____

4. One cubic puzzle is 2 inches on each side. What is the volume in cubic inches? _____

5. The factory sells a cubic flashlight which is 5 inches on each side. What is the volume? _____

6. The Cubic Factory needs to package its one-inch cubic puzzles in large boxes which are 9 inches long, 10 inches wide, and 10 inches high. How many cubic puzzles could they fit in each box?

_____

7. The factory packages its one-inch cubic magnifying glasses in boxes which are 4 inches wide, 8 inches long, and 6 inches high. How many cubic magnifying glasses could they fit into each box?

_____

8. The factory packages cubic centimeter wooden blocks in boxes which are 10 centimeters long, 10 centimeters wide, and 10 centimeters high. How many cubic centimeter blocks could they fit into each box? _____

9. The factory packages its one-cubic foot games in huge boxes which are 4 feet long, 5 feet wide, and 6 feet high. How many cubic foot games can they fit into each box? _____

10. How many one-inch cubic puzzles can the factory fit into a box which is a cubic foot (1 foot long, 1 foot wide, and 1 foot high)? _____

Practice 29

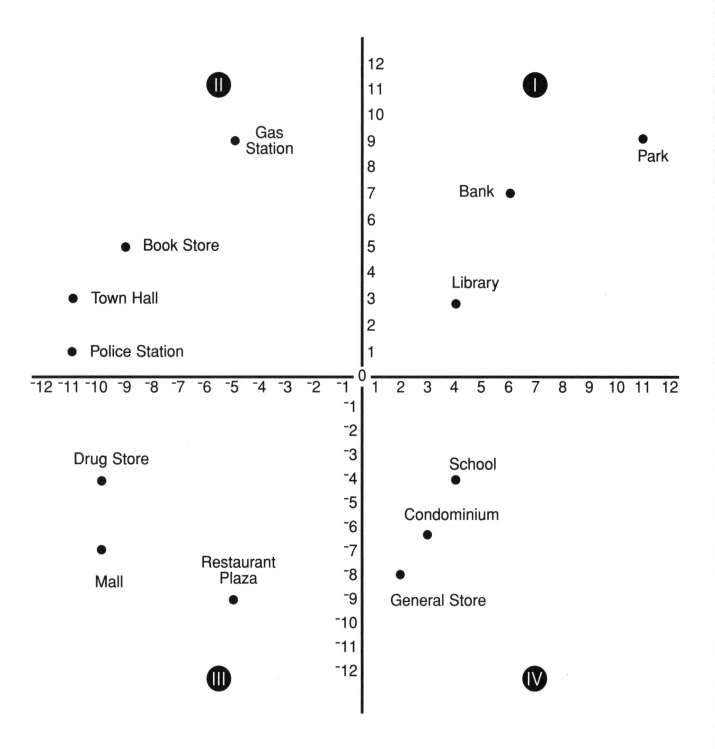

Practice 29 *(cont.)* ꙮ ꙮ ꙮ ꙮ ꙮ ꙮ ꙮ ꙮ ꙮ ꙮ ꙮ

> **Directions**
> * Study the grid shown on page 32.
> * Notice where landmarks such as the school and library are located.
> * Notice which numbers are positive and which are negative.
> * Note how the four quadrants are labeled: I, II, III, and IV.
> * Remember: Always go across before going up or down.
> * Use the information to answer these word problems.

1. What building is located at coordinates (4, 3)?_____

2. What city building is located at coordinates (⁻11, 3)? _____

3. Which business is located at (⁻5, 9)?_____

4. What are the coordinates of the police station?_____

5. What are the coordinates of the school? _____

6. What are the coordinates of the restaurant plaza?_____

7. What public area is located at coordinates (11, 9)? _____

8. What are the coordinates of the mall?_____

9. What are the coordinates of the book store? _____

10. What is located at coordinates (2, ⁻8)? _____

11. What is located at coordinates (⁻10, ⁻4)?_____

12. Which quadrant has all negative coordinates? _____

13. Which quadrant has only positive coordinates? _____

14. Which quadrant always begins with a negative number and concludes with a positive number?

_____

Labeling Coordinates

Directions: Locate and label each of the coordinate pairs listed below. Draw a straight line connecting each point to the next.

A (⁻7, ⁻10)	G (3, 6)	B (⁻5, ⁻6)	H (3, ⁻3)
C (⁻3, ⁻2)	I (3, ⁻9)	D (⁻1, 2)	J (3, ⁻10)
E (1, 6)	K (⁻2, ⁻10)	F (3, 10)	A (⁻7, ⁻10

Practice 30 ꩜ ꩜ ꩜ ꩜ ꩜ ꩜ ꩜ ꩜ ꩜ ꩜ ꩜ ꩜ ꩜

Two events are independent if the cause of one event has no relationship to the other event. To determine the probability of independent events, multiply the probability of one event occurring times the probability of the other event occurring.

Directions: Compute the probability of independent events in the following problems. The first one is done for you.

1. The probability that a student in your classroom likes ice cream is $\frac{3}{4}$. The probability that a child in your classroom likes to play football is $\frac{2}{5}$. What is the probability that a student in your classroom likes both ice cream and football? _____

   $\frac{3}{4}$ x $\frac{2}{5}$ = $\frac{3}{10}$

2. The probability that a sixth grade student in Garfield School likes purple is $\frac{1}{3}$. The probability that a sixth grade student likes pizza is $\frac{4}{5}$. What is the probability that a sixth grade student at Garfield likes both purple and pizza? _____

3. On a baseball team $\frac{9}{10}$ of the players got to hit and $\frac{1}{5}$ of the players got to pitch. What is the probability that a player got to both hit and pitch? _____

4. A group of sixth graders went to science camp where $\frac{11}{12}$ of them got to go day hiking and $\frac{3}{4}$ went night hiking. What is the probability that a sixth grader went hiking at both times?

   _____

5. In one sixth grade classroom, $\frac{3}{4}$ of the students play soccer and $\frac{2}{3}$ of the students play basketball. What is the probability that a student played both sports? _____

6. At Garfield School $\frac{1}{8}$ of the sixth grade students belong to the science club and $\frac{3}{5}$ belong to the sports club. What is the probability of a student belonging to both clubs? _____

7. In one classroom, $\frac{4}{5}$ of the boys wore tennis shoes and $\frac{5}{6}$ of the boys wore a belt. What is the probability that a boy wore both tennis shoes and a belt? _____

8. In one classroom, $\frac{4}{9}$ of the students liked chocolate cake, $\frac{2}{3}$ of the students liked ice cream, and $\frac{3}{5}$ of the students liked hot fudge. What is the probability that a student liked all three foods?

   _____

9. In one classroom, $\frac{4}{5}$ of the students liked reading, $\frac{2}{3}$ of the students liked math, and $\frac{3}{4}$ of the students liked art. What is the probability that a student liked all three subjects? _____

10. In one classroom, $\frac{1}{3}$ of the students liked broccoli, $\frac{1}{3}$ of the students liked spinach, and $\frac{1}{3}$ of the students liked cabbage. What is the probability that a student liked all three vegetables?

    _____

Practice 31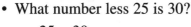

> Equations can often be written to make problem solving easier.
> - What number less 25 is 30?
> $n - 25 = 30$ $n = 55$
> - What number is 6 times 70?
> $n = 6 \times 70$ $n = 420$
> - What number divided by 4 equals 9?
> $n/4 = 9$ $n = 36$

Directions: Write an equation for each word problem. Then solve the equation. The first one is done for you.

1. What number is 12 less than 35?

   Equation: $\underline{n = 35 - 12}$

   Solution: $\underline{n = 23}$

6. What number divided by 4 equals 12?

   Equation: _____

   Solution: _____

2. What number added to 23 equals 41?

   Equation: _____

   Solution: _____

7. What number times 12 equals 96?

   Equation: _____

   Solution: _____

3. What number less 29 is 61?

   Equation: _____

   Solution: _____

8. What number divided by 8 equals 11?

   Equation: _____

   Solution: _____

4. What number added to 36 equals 53?

   Equation: _____

   Solution: _____

9. What number times 19 equals 190?

   Equation: _____

   Solution: _____

5. What number added to 19 equals 43?

   Equation: _____

   Solution: _____

10. What number divided into 42 equals 6?

    Equation: _____

    Solution: _____

Practice 32

Discount Sporting Goods has thousands of items to appeal to every taste. The store is loaded with a variety of sporting equipment. Help the owners compute these ratios.

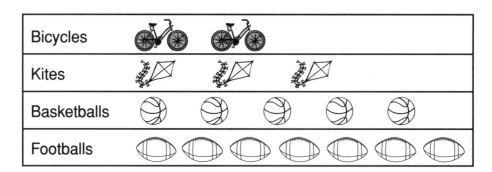

Balls	
Bats	
Mitts	
Caps	

Directions: Use the illustration to help you compute these ratios. The first one is done for you.

1. What is the ratio of baseballs to bats? _____5:4 or 5/4_____

2. What is the ratio of bats to baseballs? _____

3. What is the ratio of mitts to balls? _____

4. What is the ratio of balls to mitts? _____

5. What is the ratio of caps to balls? _____

6. What is the ratio of balls to caps? _____

7. What is the ratio of bats to caps? _____

8. What is the ratio of caps to bats? _____

Bicycles	
Kites	
Basketballs	
Footballs	

9. What is the ratio of bicycles to kites? _____

10. What is the ratio of kites to bicycles? _____

11. What is the ratio of footballs to basketballs?_____

12. What is the ratio of basketballs to footballs?_____

13. What is the ratio of kites to footballs?_____

14. What is the ratio of footballs to kites?_____

15. What is the ratio of balls to bicycles? _____

16. What is the ratio of bicycles to balls? _____

Practice 33 ♪ ☙ ♪ ☙ ♪ ☙ ♪ ☙ ♪ ☙ ♪ ☙ ♪ ♪ ☙

At Micro Models they design the exact replicas of houses, schools, businesses, sports arenas, and other structures. Help them complete the proportions in the problems below. The first one is done for you.

Reminder: To solve a proportion, the product of the means (middle terms) equals the product of the extremes (end terms).

1. Each inch of a model house represents 4 feet of a real house. How many feet are represented by 20 inches?

   Equation: 1:4 :: 20:*n so n* = 80

   Answer: 80 feet

2. One inch on a model basketball court equals 2 feet. How many feet are represented by 25 inches?

   Equation: 1:2 :: 25:n

   Answer: _____

3. On a model school, 3 centimeters represents 15 meters. How many meters are represented by 9 centimeters?

   Equation: _____

   Answer: _____

4. The height on a model skyscraper uses a scale of 4 centimeters for each story. How many stories are represented by 100 centimeters?

   Equation: _____

   Answer: _____

5. The length of a model football field represented by a scale of 3 inches for 10 yards. How many yards are represented by 33 inches?

   Equation: _____

   Answer: _____

6. The length of a model swimming pool is represented by 3 centimeters to every 10 meters. How many meters are represented by 15 centimeters?

   Equation: _____

   Answer: _____

7. The length of a road is represented by a scale of 5 inches for every 3 miles. How many inches will be used to represent 30 miles?

   Equation: _____

   Answer: _____

8. The length of 7 yards on a scale model is represented by 2 inches. How many inches would be used to represent 42 yards?

   Equation: _____

   Answer: _____

Practice 34 ∂ ☙ ∂ ☙ ∂ ☙ ∂ ☙ ∂ ∂ ☙

Students in a sixth grade classroom collected data by surveying classmates on a variety of subjects, including height, weight, grades, allowances, books read, hours spent watching TV, and other subjects. Help them compute the average for each topic.

The average is computed this way:

> • Add all of the separate values in a set of data.   • Divide by the number of units of data.
>
>   • Round to the nearest integer

1. A group of 9 boys in the classroom were measured for height. These were the heights recorded in inches: 51, 61, 57, 63, 60, 59, 60, 55, 62.

   Total: _____   Divided by: _____   Average: _____

2. A group of 11 students recorded these math scores: 88, 56, 92, 96, 100, 87, 66, 75, 81, 80, 90.

   Total: _____   Divided by: _____   Average: _____

3. These were the weights in pounds of 13 students surveyed: 88, 84, 77, 78, 90, 100, 106, 95, 96, 84, 88, 93, 81.

   Total: _____   Divided by: _____   Average: _____

4. A group of 10 students sold Valentine candy boxes during a school fund raising project. These were the number of boxes sold: 14, 20, 12, 8, 6, 3, 15, 19, 24, 17.

   Total: _____   Divided by: _____   Average: _____

5. Twelve students were surveyed on the number of books read in the last month. These were the responses: 4, 2, 1, 0, 14, 10, 5, 6, 7, 4, 5, 5.

   Total: _____   Divided by: _____   Average: _____

6. Thirteen students were surveyed on the number of hours they spent watching television in one week. These were the responses: 20, 23, 14, 7, 6, 1, 0, 15, 30, 20, 12, 8, 19.

   Total: _____   Divided by: _____   Average: _____

7. Sixteen students surveyed listed these weekly dollar allowances: 10, 9, 20, 0, 5, 1, 2, 8, 9, 5, 3, 0, 15, 14, 5, 3.

   Total: _____   Divided by: _____   Average: _____

Practice 35 ꙮ ꙮ ꙮ ꙮ ꙮ ꙮ ꙮ ꙮ ꙮ ꙮ ꙮ ꙮ ꙮ ꙮ ꙮ

The students at Garfield School measured each other's heights to the nearest inch. Help them compute the mode and median for each group below.

Follow these steps:

- Organize the numbers in order from least to greatest.

- The **mode** is the most frequently occurring number. (You can have more than one mode.)

- The **median** is the number in the middle of the numbers. (If there are two numbers in the center, add the two numbers and divide by 2.)

1. A group of 11 girls in the fifth grade recorded these heights in inches: 48, 47, 52, 54, 49, 46, 56, 50, 52, 53, 52.

   Least to Greatest: _____

   Mode: _____   Median: _____

2. A group of 13 boys in the sixth grade recorded these heights in inches: 63, 60, 57, 59, 49, 58, 59, 47, 61, 60, 56, 59, 55.

   Least to Greatest: _____

   Mode: _____   Median: _____

3. The sixth grade basketball team recorded these heights: 66, 65, 59, 57, 60, 61, 59, 63, 61, 63.

   Least to Greatest: _____

   Mode: _____   Median: _____

4. The fifth grade soccer team recorded these heights: 49, 57, 55, 53, 49, 59, 54, 52, 49, 47, 51

   Least to Greatest: _____

   Mode: _____   Median: _____

5. The student council recorded these heights: 61, 40, 44, 50, 55, 48, 39, 60, 58, 57, 45, 57, 44, 60

   Least to Greatest: _____

   Mode: _____   Median: _____

Test Practice 1 ꙮ ꙮ ꙮ ꙮ ꙮ ꙮ ꙮ ꙮ ꙮ ꙮ ꙮ ꙮ

Directions: Fill in the circle for the correct answer to each word problem.

1. Dodger Stadium seats 56,000 fans. Wrigley Field seats 38,902 fans. How many more fans can be seated in Dodger Stadium?
   - (A) 17,998
   - (B) 18,098
   - (C) 17,098
   - (D) 94,902

2. Kristin had 59 marbles. The school marble champion had 34 times as many marbles. How many marbles did the champion have?
   - (A) 2,106
   - (B) 3,006
   - (C) 2,206
   - (D) 2,006

3. Reggie Jackson had 563 career home runs. Frank Robinson had 586 career home runs, and Willie Mays had 660 career home runs. How many home runs did they have in all?
   - (A) 1,810
   - (B) 1,809
   - (C) 1,909
   - (D) 2,809

4. At Forty-one Flavors it costs $1.99 for a triple scoop of ice cream and $2.79 for a regular sundae. What is the total?
   - (A) $4.78
   - (B) $4.79
   - (C) $3.78
   - (D) $0.80

5. Every minute your bone marrow produces 3,000,000 red blood cells. How many red blood cells are made in 1 hour (60 minutes)?
   - (A) 180,000,000
   - (B) 18,000,000
   - (C) 240,000,000
   - (D) 1,800,000

6. You breathe about 23 times a minute. How many times would you breathe in 60 minutes?
   - (A) 1,390
   - (B) 1,480
   - (C) 1,380
   - (D) 2,380

7. Los Angeles has 3,694,820 people. New York City has 8,008,278 people. How many more people live in New York City?
   - (A) 5,313,458
   - (B) 4,313,458
   - (C) 4,323,468
   - (D) 11,703,108

8. Danny won a bag of 800 candies. He split them evenly among his 25 classmates. How many candies did each classmate receive?
   - (A) 30
   - (B) 33
   - (C) 25
   - (D) 32

9. An arena can seat 3,000 fans. All of the seats are sold in packages of 15 tickets. How many packages can be sold?
   - (A) 2,000
   - (B) 200
   - (C) 45,000
   - (D) 220

10. One arena holds 2,314 fans and another holds 4,567. How many fans can they seat altogether?
    - (A) 6,981
    - (B) 7,881
    - (C) 2,253
    - (D) 6,881

#3731 Practice Makes Perfect: Word Problems

Test Practice 2 ⟲ ⟲ ⟲ ⟲ ⟲ ⟲ ⟲ ⟲ ⟲ ⟲ ⟲

Directions: Fill in the circle for the correct answer to each word problem.

1. Sarah bought $\frac{1}{4}$ feet of licorice and Jenny bought $\frac{3}{8}$ feet of licorice. How much licorice did they buy in all?

   Ⓐ $\frac{4}{8}$ feet   Ⓒ $\frac{4}{12}$ feet

   Ⓑ $\frac{5}{8}$ feet   Ⓓ $\frac{1}{8}$ feet

2. A ground skink is $5\frac{1}{2}$ inches long. A Western skink is $8\frac{11}{12}$ inches long. How much longer is the Western skink?

   Ⓐ $12\frac{5}{12}$ inches

   Ⓑ $4\frac{5}{12}$ inches

   Ⓒ $3\frac{9}{10}$ inches

   Ⓓ $3\frac{5}{12}$ inches

3. Each student in a science class received $\frac{3}{4}$ ounces of water. How much water was needed for 28 students?

   Ⓐ 22 ounces

   Ⓑ 84 ounces

   Ⓒ 21 ounces

   Ⓓ 38 ounces

4. A gray wolf is $80\frac{5}{8}$ inches long. A red fox is $40\frac{1}{4}$ inches long. How much longer is the gray wolf?

   Ⓐ $40\frac{3}{8}$ inches

   Ⓑ $120\frac{7}{8}$ inches

   Ⓒ $40\frac{5}{8}$ inches

   Ⓓ $40\frac{7}{8}$ inches

5. Patti has a footprint which is $5\frac{1}{2}$ inches long. How long a line would 24 of her footprints make?

   Ⓐ 144 inches   Ⓒ $29\frac{1}{2}$ inches

   Ⓑ 264 inches   Ⓓ 132 inches

6. A line of shoeprints was 42 inches long. Each shoeprint was $3\frac{1}{2}$ inches long. How many shoeprints were in the line?

   Ⓐ 12

   Ⓑ 14

   Ⓒ $45\frac{1}{2}$

   Ⓓ 147

7. Victoria's roller racer traveled $8\frac{2}{3}$ feet in one trial and $9\frac{2}{5}$ feet in a second trial. How far did it travel in all?

   Ⓐ $17\frac{4}{15}$ feet

   Ⓑ $18\frac{14}{15}$ feet

   Ⓒ $18\frac{1}{15}$ feet

   Ⓓ $1\frac{4}{15}$ feet

8. One bag of Geodesic gumballs holds $1\frac{1}{3}$ lbs. How many pounds are in 30 bags of gumballs?

   Ⓐ 40 lbs.

   Ⓑ 10 lbs.

   Ⓒ 30 lbs.

   Ⓓ $31\frac{1}{3}$ lbs.

9. A teacher needed to cut a 24-foot rope into pieces which were $\frac{3}{4}$ feet long. How many pieces could the teacher cut?

   Ⓐ 42

   Ⓑ 32

   Ⓒ 18

   Ⓓ 31

10. A teacher had a roll of art paper $\frac{11}{12}$ feet long to cut evenly for 22 students. How long was each piece?

   Ⓐ $\frac{1}{6}$ feet   Ⓒ $\frac{1}{24}$ feet

   Ⓑ $\frac{1}{3}$ feet   Ⓓ $20\frac{1}{6}$ feet

Test Practice 3 ⟿ ⟿ ⟿ ⟿ ⟿ ⟿ ⟿ ⟿ ⟿ ⟿ ⟿

Directions: Fill in the circle for the correct answer to each word problem.

1. A fire beetle is 2.5 centimeters long. A blue bottle fly is 1.3 centimeters long. How much longer is the fire beetle?
   - Ⓐ 1.2 centimeters
   - Ⓑ 2.2 centimeters
   - Ⓒ 3.8 centimeters
   - Ⓓ 1.3 centimeters

2. An Eastern diamondback rattlesnake is 243.88 centimeters long. A second one is 91.4 centimeters long. What is their combined length?
   - Ⓐ 334.29 centimeters
   - Ⓑ 335.28 centimeters
   - Ⓒ 235.28 centimeters
   - Ⓓ 152.48 centimeters

3. A box of Grasshopper Candy Kisses weighs 12.35 ounces. How much do 12 boxes weigh?
   - Ⓐ 147.28 ounces
   - Ⓑ 128.2 ounces
   - Ⓒ 148.2 ounces
   - Ⓓ 144.35 ounces

4. The school football team won 9 of the 12 games it played. What was its winning percentage?
   - Ⓐ .800
   - Ⓑ .750
   - Ⓒ 1.330
   - Ⓓ .250

5. A sports car traveled 14.248 miles on a gallon of gas. An SUV traveled 11.03 miles on one gallon. How much farther did the sports car go?
   - Ⓐ 32.18 miles
   - Ⓑ 25.278 miles
   - Ⓒ 0.3218 miles
   - Ⓓ 3.218 miles

6. You took a 288-mile bicycle tour in 40 hours. How many miles per hour did you travel?
   - Ⓐ 72 m.p.h.
   - Ⓑ 7.2 m.p.h.
   - Ⓒ 0.72 m.p.h.
   - Ⓓ 720 m.p.h.

7. Your friend rode his skateboard 90.45 feet in one minute. How many feet can he ride in 40 minutes?
   - Ⓐ 36.18 feet
   - Ⓑ 361.8 feet
   - Ⓒ 3.618 feet
   - Ⓓ 3,618 feet

8. A box of 25 Beetle Bites costs $9.50. What is the cost of each Beetle Bite?
   - Ⓐ $9.75
   - Ⓑ $0.25
   - Ⓒ $0.38
   - Ⓓ $0.48

9. Each Sweet 'n Sour Drop costs $0.05. How many drops are in a bag costing $3.50?
   - Ⓐ 70
   - Ⓑ 75
   - Ⓒ 80
   - Ⓓ 90

10. A common iguana is 200 centimeters long. A Western fence lizard is 23.49 centimeters long. How much longer is the iguana?
   - Ⓐ 175.5 centimeters
   - Ⓑ 17.651 centimeters
   - Ⓒ 77.49 centimeters
   - Ⓓ 176.51 centimeters

 #3731 Practice Makes Perfect: Word Problems

Test Practice 4

Directions: Fill in the circle for the correct answer to each word problem.

1. A swimming pool is 21 meters wide and 50 meters long. What is the area?
   - (A) 1,150 m²
   - (B) 1,005 m²
   - (C) 1,050 m²
   - (D) 2,050 m²

2. What is the perimeter of a square kite 20 inches long on each side?
   - (A) 400 inches
   - (B) 40 inches
   - (C) 80 inches
   - (D) 200 inches

3. What is the circumference of a circle with a radius of 4 centimeters? (Use 3.14 for π.)
   - (A) 2.512 centimeters
   - (B) 25.12 centimeters
   - (C) 12.56 centimeters
   - (D) 7.14 centimeters

4. Mr. Brown's lawn is shaped like a parallelogram with a height of 12.8 yards and a base of 20 yards. What is the area?
   - (A) 286 yd.²
   - (B) 360 yd.²
   - (C) 32.8 yd.²
   - (D) 256 yd.²

5. Carissa's front lawn is shaped like a triangle with a base of 30 feet and a height of 15 feet. What is the area?
   - (A) 450 feet²
   - (B) 45 feet²
   - (C) 250 feet²
   - (D) 225 feet²

6. Matthew made a model circular parachute with a radius of 5 inches. What is the area? (Use 3.14 for π.)
   - (A) 7.85 inches²
   - (B) 78.5 inches²
   - (C) 31.4 inches²
   - (D) .785 inches²

7. A circular flower planter has a diameter of 40 inches. What is the circumference? (Use 3.14 for π.)
   - (A) 125.6 inches
   - (B) 12.56 inches
   - (C) 1.256 inches
   - (D) 1256 inches

8. What is the volume of a room which is 10 feet high, 9 feet long, and 8 feet wide?
   - (A) 7,200 feet³
   - (B) 72 feet³
   - (C) 90 feet³
   - (D) 720 feet³

9. How many one-foot cubes can fit into a box which is 12 feet high, 4 feet wide, and 6 feet long?
   - (A) 298
   - (B) 288
   - (C) 36
   - (D) 388

10. A bicycle wheel has a 13-inch radius. What is the circumference? (Use 3.14 for π.)
    - (A) 82.64 inches
    - (B) 8.164 inches
    - (C) 81.64 inches
    - (D) 91.64 inches

Test Practice 5 ⟳ ⟳ ⟳ ⟳ ⟳ ⟳ ⟳ ⟳ ⟳ ⟳ ⟳ ⟳

Directions: Fill in the circle for the correct answer to each word problem.

1. A black bag holds 7 red marbles and 4 blue marbles. What is the probability of drawing a blue marble?
   - (A) 4 in 7
   - (B) 7 in 11
   - (C) 4 in 11
   - (D) 0

2. Solve the equation. What number plus 17 equals 45?
   - (A) $n = 62$
   - (B) $n = 45$
   - (C) $n = 28$
   - (D) $n = 18$

3. In a school survey $\frac{3}{4}$ of the students liked hot dogs and $\frac{2}{3}$ of the students liked ice cream. What is the probability that a student liked both hot dogs and ice cream?
   - (A) $\frac{1}{2}$
   - (C) $\frac{1}{4}$
   - (B) $\frac{5}{7}$
   - (D) $\frac{5}{12}$

4. Solve the equation. What number divided by 5 equals 12?
   - (A) $2\frac{1}{2}$
   - (B) 60
   - (C) 10
   - (D) 80

5. A sporting goods store has 8 basketballs and 7 baseballs. What is the ratio of baseballs to basketballs?
   - (A) 7:15
   - (B) 8:7
   - (C) 15:8
   - (D) 7:8

6. In a model house 3 centimeters represents 10 feet. How many feet are represented by 12 centimeters?
   - (A) 40 feet
   - (B) 60 feet
   - (C) 120 feet
   - (D) 22 feet

7. Solve the equation. What number divided by 4 equals 13?
   - (A) $n = 17$
   - (B) $n = 48$
   - (C) $n = 52$
   - (D) $n = 26$

8. In one school, $\frac{1}{10}$ of the students belonged to the Spanish Club and $\frac{2}{7}$ participated in intramural games. What is the probability that a student participated in both the Spanish Club and intramural games?
   - (A) $\frac{2}{10}$
   - (C) $\frac{2}{35}$
   - (B) $\frac{1}{35}$
   - (D) $\frac{3}{17}$

9. Solve the equation. What number divided into 144 equals 16?
   - (A) 12
   - (B) 18
   - (C) 14
   - (D) 9

10. If 1 in 10 students are left-handed, how many students in a class of 30 would be left-handed?
    - (A) 4
    - (B) 10
    - (C) 3
    - (D) 1

Test Practice 6 🐚 🐚 🐚 🐚 🐚 🐚 🐚 🐚 🐚 🐚

Directions: Fill in the circle for the correct answer to each word problem.

1. Texas Stadium holds 65,675 Cowboys' fans. Giants' Stadium holds 79,466 fans. How many more Giants' fans can be seated?

   Ⓐ 14,791
   Ⓑ 145,141
   Ⓒ 13,791
   Ⓓ 13,991

2. Jane bought $2\frac{1}{3}$ lbs. of gumballs and $1\frac{3}{4}$ lb. of hard candy. How many pounds of candy did she buy altogether?

   Ⓐ $4\frac{1}{12}$ lbs.
   Ⓑ $3\frac{11}{12}$ lbs.
   Ⓒ $4\frac{11}{12}$ lbs.
   Ⓓ $3\frac{4}{7}$ lbs.

3. Tara can read 2 pages in 3 minutes. How many pages can she read in 60 minutes?

   Ⓐ 50
   Ⓑ 40
   Ⓒ 60
   Ⓓ 20

4. A leafhopper is $^3/_8$ inches long. How long would a line of 24 leafhoppers stretch?

   Ⓐ 12 inches
   Ⓑ 10 inches
   Ⓒ $24\frac{3}{8}$ inches
   Ⓓ 9 inches

5. What is the sum of ⁻19 and ⁻37?

   Ⓐ ⁻66
   Ⓑ ⁻56
   Ⓒ ⁻18
   Ⓓ ⁺18

6. A lawn is shaped like a triangle with a height of 14 feet and a base of 32 feet. What is the area of the lawn?

   Ⓐ 234 feet²
   Ⓑ 448 feet²
   Ⓒ 224 feet²
   Ⓓ 46 feet²

7. A box is 7 inches long, 5 inches wide, and 10 inches high. What is the volume of the box?

   Ⓐ 350 inches³
   Ⓑ 22 inches³
   Ⓒ 35 inches³
   Ⓓ 360 inches³

8. Determine the mode in this set: (9, 4, 6, 9, 3, 7, 9, 6).

   Ⓐ 6
   Ⓑ 9
   Ⓒ 6.5
   Ⓓ 7

9. James attempted 12 shots and made 9 shots. What was his shooting percentage?

   Ⓐ 25%
   Ⓑ 75%
   Ⓒ 133%
   Ⓓ 100%

10. Tony drove 400 miles from Los Angeles to San Francisco in 8 hours. What was his rate of speed?

    Ⓐ 408 m.p.h.
    Ⓑ 60 m.p.h.
    Ⓒ 40.5 m.p.h.
    Ⓓ 50 m.p.h.

Answer Sheet

Test Practice 1

1. Ⓐ Ⓑ Ⓒ Ⓓ
2. Ⓐ Ⓑ Ⓒ Ⓓ
3. Ⓐ Ⓑ Ⓒ Ⓓ
4. Ⓐ Ⓑ Ⓒ Ⓓ
5. Ⓐ Ⓑ Ⓒ Ⓓ
6. Ⓐ Ⓑ Ⓒ Ⓓ
7. Ⓐ Ⓑ Ⓒ Ⓓ
8. Ⓐ Ⓑ Ⓒ Ⓓ
9. Ⓐ Ⓑ Ⓒ Ⓓ
10. Ⓐ Ⓑ Ⓒ Ⓓ

Test Practice 2

1. Ⓐ Ⓑ Ⓒ Ⓓ
2. Ⓐ Ⓑ Ⓒ Ⓓ
3. Ⓐ Ⓑ Ⓒ Ⓓ
4. Ⓐ Ⓑ Ⓒ Ⓓ
5. Ⓐ Ⓑ Ⓒ Ⓓ
6. Ⓐ Ⓑ Ⓒ Ⓓ
7. Ⓐ Ⓑ Ⓒ Ⓓ
8. Ⓐ Ⓑ Ⓒ Ⓓ
9. Ⓐ Ⓑ Ⓒ Ⓓ
10. Ⓐ Ⓑ Ⓒ Ⓓ

Test Practice 3

1. Ⓐ Ⓑ Ⓒ Ⓓ
2. Ⓐ Ⓑ Ⓒ Ⓓ
3. Ⓐ Ⓑ Ⓒ Ⓓ
4. Ⓐ Ⓑ Ⓒ Ⓓ
5. Ⓐ Ⓑ Ⓒ Ⓓ
6. Ⓐ Ⓑ Ⓒ Ⓓ
7. Ⓐ Ⓑ Ⓒ Ⓓ
8. Ⓐ Ⓑ Ⓒ Ⓓ
9. Ⓐ Ⓑ Ⓒ Ⓓ
10. Ⓐ Ⓑ Ⓒ Ⓓ

Test Practice 4

1. Ⓐ Ⓑ Ⓒ Ⓓ
2. Ⓐ Ⓑ Ⓒ Ⓓ
3. Ⓐ Ⓑ Ⓒ Ⓓ
4. Ⓐ Ⓑ Ⓒ Ⓓ
5. Ⓐ Ⓑ Ⓒ Ⓓ
6. Ⓐ Ⓑ Ⓒ Ⓓ
7. Ⓐ Ⓑ Ⓒ Ⓓ
8. Ⓐ Ⓑ Ⓒ Ⓓ
9. Ⓐ Ⓑ Ⓒ Ⓓ
10. Ⓐ Ⓑ Ⓒ Ⓓ

Test Practice 5

1. Ⓐ Ⓑ Ⓒ Ⓓ
2. Ⓐ Ⓑ Ⓒ Ⓓ
3. Ⓐ Ⓑ Ⓒ Ⓓ
4. Ⓐ Ⓑ Ⓒ Ⓓ
5. Ⓐ Ⓑ Ⓒ Ⓓ
6. Ⓐ Ⓑ Ⓒ Ⓓ
7. Ⓐ Ⓑ Ⓒ Ⓓ
8. Ⓐ Ⓑ Ⓒ Ⓓ
9. Ⓐ Ⓑ Ⓒ Ⓓ
10. Ⓐ Ⓑ Ⓒ Ⓓ

Test Practice 6

1. Ⓐ Ⓑ Ⓒ Ⓓ
2. Ⓐ Ⓑ Ⓒ Ⓓ
3. Ⓐ Ⓑ Ⓒ Ⓓ
4. Ⓐ Ⓑ Ⓒ Ⓓ
5. Ⓐ Ⓑ Ⓒ Ⓓ
6. Ⓐ Ⓑ Ⓒ Ⓓ
7. Ⓐ Ⓑ Ⓒ Ⓓ
8. Ⓐ Ⓑ Ⓒ Ⓓ
9. Ⓐ Ⓑ Ⓒ Ⓓ
10. Ⓐ Ⓑ Ⓒ Ⓓ

Answer Key

Page 4
1. 279 marbles
2. 146 marbles
3. 188 marbles
4. 55 marbles
5. 1,316 marbles
6. 37 marbles
7. 96 marbles
8. 222 marbles
9. 245 marbles
10. 468 marbles
11. 71 marbles
    12 marbles
12. 444 marbles

Page 5
1. addition
   19,056 bases
2. subtraction
   1,689 at bats
3. addition
   2,129 home runs
4. division
   177 hits
5. multiplication
   3,928,500 tickets
6. subtraction
   1,578 strike outs
7. division
   2,800 groups
8. subtraction
   329 walks
9. division
   175 hits (174 R13)
10. division
    .600 or 60%

Page 6
1. subtraction
   37,036 people
2. subtraction
   14,443 people
3. addition
   132,118 fans
4. addition
   35,292 fans
5. division
   860 packages
6. division
   2,000 packages
7. subtraction
   28,538 fans
8. division
   8,250 packages
9. multiplication
   601,536 fans
10. multiplication
    3,649,050 tickets

Page 7
1. 7/12 lb.
2. 1 5/12 lb.
3. 1/8 lb.
4. 1/12 lb.
5. 5 lb.
6. 1/4 feet
7. 1 7/10 lb.
8. 11/24 feet
9. 6 cups
10. 1 19/30 lb.

Page 8
1. 15 ounces
2. 24 3/4 ounces
3. 21/40 ounces
4. 25 students
5. 14 students
6. 1/12 ounces
7. 1 7/10 ounces
8. 27 1/5 ounces
9. 9 3/8 ounces
10. 8 3/4 lb.
11. 1 1/2 ounces
12. 28 cups

Page 9
1. 10 3/8 inches
2. 32 3/4 inches
3. 7/8 inches
4. 51 5/8 inches
5. 83 7/8 inches
6. 3 1/4 lb.
7. 20 1/4 lb.
8. 24 1/6 inches
9. 14 1/8 ounces
10. 20 3/8 inches

Page 10
1. 76 inches
2. 52 1/5 inches
3. 10 prints
4. 8 prints
5. 150 inches
6. 355 inches
7. 23 1/3 inches
8. 7 prints
9. 451 inches
10. 8 prints

Page 11
1. 2 1/4 feet
2. 9 5/6 feet
3. 17 3/4 feet
4. 3 1/8 feet
5. 2 1/3 feet
6. 6 2/5 times
7. 12 lengths
8. 6 1/12 feet
9. 5 1/2 feet
10. 14 7/12 feet

Page 12
1. $5.04
2. $0.56
3. $63.68
4. $43.45
5. $5.51
6. $5.04
7. $29.25
8. $0.96
9. $10.13
10. $20.15
11. $18.35
12. $17.10

Page 13
1. 7.9 centimeters
2. 87.6 centimeters
3. 30.25 centimeters
4. 220.89 centimeters
5. 204.26 centimeters
6. 347.863 centimeters
7. 24.99 centimeters
8. 1.201 centimeters
9. 56.899 centimeters
10. 59.663 centimeters
11. 26.989 centimeters
12. 181.91 centimeters

Page 14
1. 0.21 lb.
2. 100.2 ounces
3. 1.09 ounces
4. 10.2 candies
5. 45.1 lb.
6. 80.5 ants
7. 969.624 ounces
8. $0.23
9. $0.38
10. 157.68 lb.

Page 15
1. 75%   6. 80%
2. 72%   7. 64%
3. 75%   8. 67%
4. 60%   9. 70%
5. 75%   10. 82%

Page 16
1. $34.00
2. $4.00
3. $1.32
4. $9.52
5. $7.00
6. $2.48
7. $15.20
8. $4.00
9. $18.00
   $42.00
10. $5.24
    $29.71

Page 17
1. 467.476 mi.
2. 2,246.8 mi.
3. 32.422 feet
4. 94.14 mi.
5. 15.23 mi.
6. 44.636 mi.
7. 177.813 m.p.h.
8. 3,030.957 lb.
9. 91.05 mi.
10. 880.431 mi.

Page 18
1. 60 m.p.h.
2. 50 m.p.h.
3. 30 m.p.h.
4. 60 m.p.h.
5. 50 m.p.h.
6. 55 m.p.h.
7. 52 m.p.h.
8. 40 m.p.h.
9. 40 m.p.h.
10. 80 m.p.h.

Page 19
1. 3,200 feet
2. 40 min.
3. 10,000 feet
4. 7,128 feet
5. 396 min.
6. 7,740 feet
7. 24,000 feet
8. 503 min.
9. 410 min.
10. 30,400 feet

Page 20
1. $1
2. $1
3. $11
4. 7
5. $21
6. 2
7. $6
8. -24
9. 17
10. -72
11. -32
12. $226

Page 21
1. $12
2. $20
3. +42
4. $7
5. -9
6. +10
7. $270
8. +156
9. -64

10. +5
11. $5
12. +20

Page 22
1. camel
2. dog/cat/red fox
3. 5 yr.
4. pig
5. 17 yr.
6. 15 yr.
7. 4 yr.
8. 9 yr.
9. 55 yr.
10. 70 yr.

Page 23
1. 30%
2. 5th/8th
3. 60%
4. no
5. 45%
6. 40%

Page 24
1. 1960
2. 1990–2000
3. 1960
4. 1950–1960
5. 1990–2000
6. 1970–1980
7. 1960–1970
8. the same
9. 10/11
10. 12/13
11. 16
12. 7/8/9
13. taller
14. 14

Page 25
1. 6   *Frequency*
2. 1   Cat 8
3. 4   Dog 12
4. 5   Snake 2
5. 2   Bird 3
6. 11   Mouse 3
7. 18   Hamster 4
8. 2   Fish 6
9. 4   Other 3
10. dog
11. snake
12. 5
13. 41
14. 27

Page 26
1. 20 m.p.h.
2. the scale starts at 20
   rather than 0

3. no
4. 5 m.p.h.
5. 35 m.p.h.
6. the scale doesn't go 0 to 70
7. start at 0/use a different scale
8. 1995
9. 1998
10. 10 thousand dollars
11. the scale is distorted, starts at 40
12. 25 thousand dollars
13. scale starts at 40 thousand dollars
14. starts at 0 and go to 70

Page 27
1. 920 feet
   48,000 feet^2
2. 288 feet
   4,700 feet^2
3. 360 feet
   8,100 feet^2
4. 600 feet
   20,000 feet^2
5. 320 yd.
   6,000 yd.^{2}
6. 260 feet
   4,225 feet^2
7. 346 m
   7,300 m^2
8. 350 yd.
   7,150 yd.^{2}

Page 28
1. 240 feet^2
2. 450 feet^2.
3. 1,035 feet^2
4. 240 feet^2
5. 4,171 feet^2
6. 1,155 feet^2
7. 672 feet^2
8. 87.5 feet^2
9. 99.6 feet^2
10. 484 feet^2

Page 29
1. C = πd
   C = 3.14 x 9
   28.26 centimeters
2. C = πd
   C = 3.14 x 23
   72.22 centimeters
3. C = 2πr
   C = 2 x 3.14 x 5
   31.4 centimeters
4. C = πd

C = 3.14 x 2
6.28 centimeters
5. C = πd
   C = 3.14 x 2.6
   8.164 centimeters
6. C = 2πr
   C = 2 x 3.14 x 12
   75.36 inches
7. C = 2πr
   C = 2 x 3.14 x 2
   12.56 inches
8. C = 2πr
   C = 2 x 3.14 x 3
   18.84 centimeters

Page 30
1. A = πr^2
   A = 3 x 3 x 3.14
   28.26 cm^2
2. A = πr^2
   A = 3.14 x 8 x 8
   200.96 inches^2
3. A = πr^2
   A = 3.14 x 6 x 6
   113.04 cm^2
4. A = πr^2
   A = 3.14 x 7 x 7
   153.86 millimeters^2
5. A = πr^2
   A = 3.14 x 9 x 9
   254.34 millimeters^2
6. A = πr^2
   A = 3.14 x 2 x 2
   12.56 feet^2
7. A = πr^2
   A = 3.14 x 4 x 4
   50.24 feet^2
8. A = πr^2
   A = 3.14 x 4.5 x 4.5
   63.585 cm^2
9. A = πr^2
   A = 3.14 x 3.5 x 3.5
   38.465 cm^2
10. A = πr^2
    A = 3.14 x 1.15 x 1.15
    4.15265 cm^2

Page 31
1. 216 inches^3
2. 27 cm^3
3. 729 inches^3
4. 8 inches^3
5. 125 inches^3
6. 900 cubic puzzles
7. 192 cubic

magnifying glasses
8. 1,000 cm^3 blocks
9. 120 games
10. 1,728 cubic puzzles

Page 33
1. library
2. town hall
3. gas station
4. (-11, 1)
5. (4, -4)
6. (-5, -9)
7. park
8. (-10, -7)
9. (-9, 5)
10. general store
11. drug store
12. III
13. I
14. II

Page 34
1. 3/10   6. 3/40
2. 4/15   7. 2/3
3. 9/50   8. 8/45
4. 11/16   9. 2/5
5. 1/2   10. 1/27

Page 35
1. $n = 35 - 12$
   $n = 23$
2. $23 + n = 41$
   $n = 18$
3. $n - 29 = 61$
   $n = 90$
4. $36 + n = 53$
   $n = 17$
5. $19 + n = 43$
   $n = 24$
6. $n/4 = 12$
   $n = 48$
7. $n \times 12 = 96$
   $n = 8$
8. $n/8 = 11$
   $n = 88$
9. $n \times 19 = 190$
   $n = 10$
10. $42/n = 6$
    $n = 7$

Page 36
1. 5:4 or 5/4
2. 4:5 or 4/5
3. 2:5 or 2/5
4. 5:2 or 5/2
5. 3:5 or 3/5
6. 5:3 or 5/3
7. 4:3 or 4/3
8. 3:4 or 3/4
9. 2:3 or 2/3

10. 3:2 or 3/2
11. 7:5 or 7/5
12. 5:7 or 5/7
13. 3:7 or 3/7
14. 7:3 or 7/3
15. 12:2 or 12/2 or 6:1 or 6/1
16. 2:12 or 2/12 or 1:6 or 1/6
17. 3:7 or 3/7
18. 7:3 or 7/3

Page 37
1. 1:4 :: 20:n
   $n = 80$ feet
2. 1:2 :: 25:n
   $n = 50$ feet
3. 3:15 :: 9:n
   $n = 45$ m
4. 4:1 :: 100:n
   $n = 25$ stories
5. 3:10 :: 33:n
   $n = 110$ yd.
6. 3:10 :: 15:n
   $n = 50$ m
7. 5:3 :: n:30
   $n = 50$ inches
8. 7:2 :: 42:n or
   2:7 :: n:42
   $n = 12$ inches

Page 38
1. 528
   9
   59 (58.67)
2. 911
   11
   83 (82.8)
3. 1,160
   13
   89 (89.2)
4. 138
   10
   14 (13.8)
5. 63
   12
   5 (5.25)
6. 175
   13
   13 (13.46)
7. 109
   16
   7 (6.8)

Page 39
1. (46, 47, 48, 49, 50, 52, 52, 52, 53, 54, 56)
   52

52
2. (47, 49, 55, 56, 57, 58, 59, 59, 59, 60, 60, 61, 63)
   59
   59
3. (57, 59, 59, 60, 61, 61, 63, 63, 65, 66)
   59, 61, 63
   61
4. (47, 49, 49, 49, 51, 52, 53, 54, 55, 57, 59)
   49
   52
5. (39, 40, 44, 44, 45, 48, 50, 55, 57, 57, 58, 60, 60, 61)
   44, 57, 60
   52.5

Page 40
1. C   6. C
2. D   7. B
3. B   8. D
4. A   9. B
5. A   10. D

Page 41
1. B   6. A
2. D   7. C
3. C   8. A
4. A   9. B
5. D   10. C

Page 42
1. A   6. B
2. B   7. D
3. C   8. C
4. B   9. A
5. D   10. D

Page 43
1. C   6. B
2. C   7. A
3. B   8. D
4. D   9. B
5. D   10. C

Page 44
1. C   6. A
2. C   7. C
3. A   8. B
4. B   9. D
5. D   10. C

Page 45
1. C   6. C
2. A   7. A
3. B   8. B
4. D   9. B
5. B   10. D